Day by Day

Books by ROBERT LOWELL

Selected Poems (1976)
The Dolphin (1973)
History (1973)
For Lizzie and Harriet (1973)
Notebook (1969) (Revised and expanded edition, 1970)
Prometheus Bound (1969)
The Voyage & other versions of poems by Baudelaire (1969)
Near the Ocean (1967)
The Old Glory (1965)
For the Union Dead (1964)
Imitations (1961)
Phaedra (translation) (1961)
Life Studies (1959)
The Mills of the Kavanaughs (1951)
Lord Weary's Castle (1946)
Land of Unlikeness (1944)

Day by Day

ROBERT LOWELL

Farrar, Straus and Giroux
New York

Copyright © 1975, 1976, 1977 by Robert Lowell
All rights reserved
Printed in the United States of America
Published in Canada by HarperCollins*CanadaLtd*
Designed by Karen Watt

Fourth printing, 1992

Some poems in this book were originally published
in somewhat different form in the following
magazines: *American Poetry Review, New York
Review of Books, Ploughshares, Salmagundi,* and
Shenandoah.

Title-page drawing by Francis Parker

Library of Congress Cataloging in Publication Data
Lowell, Robert.   Day by day.   Poems.   I. Title.
PS3523.089D39   1977   811'.5'2   77-6799

Contents

II

III

APPENDIX   *Translations*

Part One

Ulysses and Circe

I

Ten years before Troy, ten years before Circe—
things changed to the names he gave them,
then lost their names:
Myrmidons, Spartans, soldier of dire Ulysses . . .
Why should I renew his infamous sorrow?
He had his part, he thought of building
the wooden horse as big as a house
and ended the ten years' war.
"By force of fraud," he says, "I did
what neither Diomedes, nor Achilles son of Thetis,
nor the Greeks with their thousand ships . . .
I destroyed Troy."

II

What is more uxorious than waking at five
with the sun and three hours free?
He sees the familiar bluish-brown river
dangle down her flat young forearm,
then crisscross. The sun rises,
a red bonfire,
weakly rattling in the lower branches—
that eats like a locust and leaves the tree entire.
In ten minutes perhaps,
or whenever he next wakes up,
the sun is white as it mostly is,
dull changer of night to day,
itself unchanged, in war or peace.
The blinds give
bars of sunlight, bars of shade,
but the latter predominate
over the sincerity of her sybaritic bed.
She lies beside him,

a delicious, somnolent log. She says,
"Such wonderful things are being said to me—
I'm such an old sleeper, I can't respond."

III

O that morning might come without the day—
he lies awake and fears the servants,
the civilities
of their savage, assiduous voices.
It's out of hand . . . her exotic palace
spun in circles no sober Greek can navigate.
He is afraid the whining, greasy animals
who bury chewed meat beneath his window
are only human, and will claim
his place of honor on the couch.
His heart is swallowed in his throat;
it is only an ache of the mind,
the twilight of early morning . . .
"Why am I my own fugitive,
because her beauty
made me feel as other men?"

IV

She stands, her hair
intricate and winding as her heart.
They talk like two guests
waiting for the other
to leave the house—
her mongrel harmony
of the irreconcilable.
Here his derelict choice
changes to necessity;
compassion is terror,
no schism can split
the ruthless openness

4

of her yielding character.
Her eyes well,
and hypnotize
his followers,
the retarded animals.
They cannot stay awake,
and keep their own hours,
like degenerates
drinking the day in,
sweating it out in hysterical submission.

Young,
he made strategic choices;
in middle age he accepts
his unlikely life to come;
he will die like others as the gods will,
drowning his last crew
in uncharted ocean,
seeking the unpeopled world beyond the sun,
lost in the uproarious rudeness of a great wind.

On Circe's small island,
he grew from narrowness—
by pettiness,
he ennobled himself to fit the house.
He dislikes everything
in his impoverished life of myth.

The lotus brings a nostalgia
for the no-quarter duels he hated;
but she is only where she is.
Her speech is spiced with the faded slang
of a generation younger than his—
now the patois of the island.
Her great season goes with her;
the gorgeous girls she knew

are still her best friends,
their reputations lost like Helen's,
saved by her grace.

She is a snipper-off'er—
her discards lie about the floors,
the unused, the misused,
seacoats and insignia,
the beheaded beast.

She wants her house askew—
kept keys to lost locks,
unidentifiable portraits, dead things
wrapped in paper the color of dust . . .

the surge of the wine before the quarrel.

Slight pleasantries leave lasting burns—
the air in the high hall simmers
in the cracked beams with a thousand bugs;
though this is mid-autumn,
the moment when insects die
instantly as one would ask of a friend.

On his walk to the ship,
a solitary tree suddenly
drops half its leaves;
they stay green on the ground.
Other trees hold. In a day or two,
their leaves also will fall,
like his followers,
stained by their hesitation
prematurely brown.

V

"Long awash and often touching bottom
by the sea's great green go-light
I found my exhaustion
the light of the world.

Earth isn't earth
if my eyes are on the moon,
her likeness caught
in the split-second of vacancy—

duplicitous,
open to all men, unfaithful.

After so many millennia,
Circe,
are you tired
of turning swine to swine?

How can I please you,
if I am not a man?

I have grown bleak-boned with survival—
I who hoped to leave the earth
younger than I came.

Age is the bilge
we cannot shake from the mop.

Age walks on our faces—
at the tunnel's end,
if faith can be believed,
our flesh will grow lighter."

VI

Penelope

Ulysses circles—
neither his son's weakness,
nor passion for his wife,
which might have helped her, held him.
She sees no feat
in his flight or his flight back—
ten years to and ten years fro.
On foot and visible,
he walks from Long Wharf home.
Nobody in Ithaca knows him,
and yet he is too much remarked.
His knees run quicker than his feet,
his held-in mouth is puffy,
his eye is a traveled welcomer.
He looks for his lighthouse,
once so aggressively white—
a landmark, now a marina.
How white faced and unlucky-looking
he was twenty years ago,
even on the eve of his embarkation
and carnival of glory,
when he enticed Penelope
to dance herself to coma in his arms.
Risk was his métier.
His dusty, noontime road is home now;
he imagines her dashing to him
in the eager sacklike shift
she wore her last month pregnant.
Her then unspectacled eyes were stars—
a cornered rabbit . . . Today his house
is more convivial and condescending;
she is at home,
well furnished with her entourage,
her son, her son's friends, her lovers—

the usual chaos of living well,
health and wealth in clashing outfits—
only infirmity could justify
the deformity . . .
He has seen the known world,
the meanness and beacons of men;
the full heat of his pilgrimage
assumes the weight
and gravity of being alive.
He enters the house,
eyes shut, mouth loose.
The conjugal bed is just a step;
he mistakes
a daughter for her mother.
It is not surprising.
The men move him away—
a foolish but evil animal.
He is outdoors;
his uninvited hands are raw, they say
I love you through the locked window.
At forty, she is still
the best bosom in the room.
He looks at her,
she looks at him admiring her,
then turns to the suitors—knowing
the lying art of the divine Minerva
will not make him
invincible as he was,
her life ago, or young . . .
Volte-face—
he circles as a shark circles
visibly behind the window—
flesh-proud, sore-eyed, scar-proud,
a vocational killer
in the machismo of senility,
foretasting the apogee of mayhem—
breaking water to destroy his wake.

He is oversize. To her suitors,
he is Tom, Dick, or Harry—
his gills are pleated and aligned—
unnatural ventilation-vents
closed by a single lever
like cells in a jail—
ten years fro and ten years to.

Homecoming

What was is . . . since 1930;
the boys in my old gang
are senior partners. They start up
bald like baby birds
to embrace retirement.

At the altar of surrender,
I met you
in the hour of credulity.
How your misfortune came out clearly
to us at twenty.

At the gingerbread casino,
how innocent the nights we made it
on our *Vesuvio* martinis
with no vermouth but vodka
to sweeten the dry gin—

the lash across my face
that night we adored . . .
soon every night and all,
when your sweet, amorous
repetition changed.

Fertility is not to the forward,
or beauty to the precipitous—
things gone wrong
clothe summer
with gold leaf.

Sometimes
I catch my mind
circling for you with glazed eye—
my lost love hunting
your lost face.

Summer to summer,
the poplars sere
in the glare—
it's a town for the young,
they break themselves against the surf.

No dog knows my smell.

Last Walk?

That unhoped-for Irish sunspoiled April day
heralded the day before
by corkscrews of the eternal
whirling snow that melts and dies
and leaves the painted green pasture marsh—
and the same green ... We could even imagine
we enjoyed our life's great change then—
hand in hand with balmy smiles
graciously belittling our headlong reverse.

We walked to an artificial pond
dammed at both ends to reflect the Castle—
a natural composition for the faded colorist
on calm bright days or brighter nights.
At first we mistook the pond for a lull in the river—
the Liffey, torrential, wild,
accelerated to murder,
wider here than twenty miles downhill to Dublin—
black, rock-kneed, crashing on crags—
by excessive courage married to the ocean.

"Those swans," you said, "if one loses its mate,
the other dies. This spring a Persian exile
killed one cruelly, and its mate
refused to be fed—
It roused an explosion of xenophobia
when it died."
Explosion is growing common here;
yet everything about the royal swan
is silly, overstated, a luxury toy
beyond the fortunate child's allowance.

We sat and watched a mother swan
enthroned like a colossal head of Pharaoh
on her messy double goose-egg nest of sticks.
The male swan had escaped
their safe, stagnant, matriarchal pond
and gallanted down the stout-enriched rapids to Dublin,
smirking drunkenly, racing bumping,
as if to show a king had a right to be too happy.

I meant to write about our last walk.
We had nothing to do but gaze—
seven years, now nothing but a diverting smile,
dalliance by a river, a speeding swan . . .
the misleading promise
to last with joy as long as our bodies,
nostalgia pulverized by thought,
nomadic as yesterday's whirling snow,
all whiteness splotched.

Suicide

You only come in the tormenting
hallucinations of the night,
when my sleeping, prophetic mind
experiences things
that have not happened yet.

Sometimes in dreams
my hair came out in tufts
from my scalp,
I saw it lying there
loose on my pillow like flax.

Sometimes in dreams
my teeth got loose in my mouth . . .
Tinker, Tailor, Sailor, Sailor—
they were cherrystones,
as I spat them out.

I will not come again to you,
and risk the help I fled—
the doctors and darkness and dogs,
the hide and seek for me—
"Cuckoo, cuckoo. Here I am . . ."

If I had lived
and could have forgotten
that eventually it had to happen,
even to children—
it would have been otherwise.

One light, two lights, three—
it's day, no light is needed.
Your car I watch for never comes,
you will not see me peeping for you
behind my furtively ajar front door.

The trees close branches and redden,
their winter skeletons are hard to find;
a friend seldom seen
is not the same—
how quickly even bad cooking eats up a day.

I go to the window,
and even open it wide—
five floors down, the trees are bushes and weeds,
too contemptible and small
to delay a sparrow's fall.

Why haven't you followed me here,
as you followed me everywhere else?
You cannot do it
with vague fatality
or muffled but lethal sighs.

Do I deserve credit
for not having tried suicide—
or am I afraid
the exotic act
will make me blunder,

not knowing error
is remedied by practice,
as our first home-photographs,
headless, half-headed, tilting
extinguished by a flashbulb?

Departure

(Intermissa, Venus, diu)

"Waiting out the rain,
but what are you waiting for?
The storm can only stop
to get breath to begin again . . .
always in suspense to hit
the fugitive in flight.
Your clothes, moth-holed
with round cigarette burns,
sag the closet-pole.
Your books are rows of hollow suits;
'Who lives in them?'
we ask acidly,
and bring them down
flapping their paper wrappers.
So many secondary troubles,
the body's curative diversions;
but what does it matter,
if one is oneself, has something
past criticism to change to?
Not now as you were young . . .
Horace in his fifties held
a Ligurian girl
captive in the sleep of night,
followed her flying across the grass
of the Campus Martius, saw her lost
in the Tiber he could not hold.
Can you hear my first voice,
amused in sorrow,
dramatic in amusement . . .
catastrophies of description
knowing when to stop,
when not to stop?

It cannot be replayed;
only by exaggeration
could I tell the truth.
For me, neither boy
nor woman was a help.
Caught in the augmenting storm,
choice itself is wrong,
nothing said or not said tells—
a shapeless splatter of grounded rain . . .
Why, Love, why, are a few tears
scattered on my cheeks?"

Part Two

Our Afterlife I

[FOR PETER TAYLOR]

Southbound—
a couple in passage,
two Tennessee cardinals
in green December outside the window
dart and tag and mate—
young as they want to be.
We're not.
Since my second fatherhood
and stay in England,
I am a generation older.
We are dangerously happy—
our book-bled faces
streak like red birds,
dart unstably,
ears cocked to catch
the first shy whisper of deafness.
This year killed
Pound, Wilson, Auden . . .
promise has lost its bloom,
the inheritor reddens
like a false rose—
nodding, nodding, nodding.
Peter, in our boyish years,
30 to 40,
when Cupid was still the Christ of love's religion,
time stood on its hands.

Sleight of hand.

We drink in the central heat
to keep the cold wave out.
The stifled telephone that rings in my ear
doesn't exist.
After fifty,
the clock can't stop,
each saving breath
takes something. This is riches:
the eminence not to be envied,
the account
accumulating layer and angle,
face and profile,
50 years of snapshots,
the ladder of ripening likeness.

We are things thrown in the air
alive in flight . . .
our rust the color of the chameleon.

Our Afterlife II

Leaving a taxi at Victoria,
I saw my own face
in sharper focus and smaller
watching me from a puddle
or something I held—*your* face
on the cover of your *Collected Stories*
seamed with dread and smiling—
old short-haired poet
of the first Depression,
now back in currency.

My thinking is talking to you—
last night I fainted at dinner
and came nearer to your sickness,
nearer to the angels in nausea.
The room turned upside-down,
I was my interrupted sentence,
a misdirection tumbled back alive
on a low, cooling black table.

The doctors come more thickly,
they use exact language
even when they disagree on the mal-diagnosis
in the surgeon's feather-touch.

Were we ever weaned
from our reactionary young masters
by the *schadenfreude* of new homes?

America once lay uncropped and golden,
it left no tarnish on our windshield . . .
In a generation born under Prohibition,
the Red Revolution, the Crash,
cholesterol and bootleg—

we were artisans
retained as if we were workers
by the charities of free enterprise.

Our loyalty to one another sticks like love . . .

This year for the first time,
even cows seem transitory—
1974
of the Common Market,
the dwarf Norman appletree
espaliered to a wall.
The old boys drop like wasps
from windowsill and pane.
In a church,
the Psalmist's glass mosaic Shepherd
and bright green pastures
seem to wait
with the modish faithlessness
and erotic daydream
of art nouveau for our funeral.

Louisiana State University in 1940

[FOR ROBERT PENN WARREN]

The torch-pipes wasting waste gas all night,
O Baton Rouge, your measureless student prospects,
rats as long as my forearm regrouping toward
the sewage cleansing on the open canals—
the moisture mossing in the green seminar room
where we catnapped,
while Robert Penn Warren talked three hours
on Machiavelli . . . the tyrannicide
of princes, Cesare Borgia, Huey Long,
citing fifty English and Italian sources—
our dog-eat-dog days in isolationist America,
devouring Stalin's unmeasured retreats,
as if we had a conscience to be impartial.

"How can you beat a country
where every boy of twelve can fix a motorcycle?"
Red, you could make friends with anyone,
criminals, or even showy writer giants
you slaughtered in a review . . .

my dangerous ad hominem simplifications.

Your reminiscences have more color than life—
but because, unlike you, I'm neither novelist
nor critic, I choose your poetry:
Terror, Pursuit, Brother to Dragons, Or Else.
Can poetry get away with murder,
its terror a seizure of the imagination
foreign to our stubborn common health?
It's the authentic will to spoil,
the voice,
haunted not lost,

that lives by breaking in
berserk with inspiration,
not to be shaken without great injury,
not to be quieted by ingenious plotting—
the muse,
"rattling her crutch that puts forth a small bloom, perhaps
    white . . ."
an old master still engaging the dazzled disciple.

For John Berryman

(After reading his last Dream Song*)*

The last years we only met
when you were on the road,
and lit up for reading
your battering *Dream*—
audible, deaf . . .
in another world then as now.
I used to want to live
to avoid your elegy.
Yet really we had the same life,
the generic one
our generation offered
(*Les Maudits*—the compliment
each American generation
pays itself in passing):
first students, then with our own,
our galaxy of grands maîtres,
our fifties' fellowships
to Paris, Rome and Florence,
veterans of the Cold War not the War—
all the best of life . . .
then daydreaming to drink at six,
waiting for the iced fire,
even the feel of the frosted glass,
like waiting for a girl . . .
if you had waited.
We asked to be obsessed with writing,
and we were.

Do you wake dazed like me,
and find your lost glasses in a shoe?

Something so heavy lies on my heart—
there, still here, the good days
when we sat by a cold lake in Maine,
talking about the *Winter's Tale*,
Leontes' jealousy
in Shakespeare's broken syntax.
You got there first.
Just the other day,
I discovered how we differ—humor . . .
even in this last *Dream Song*,
to mock your catlike flight
from home and classes—
to leap from the bridge.

Girls will not frighten the frost from the grave.

To my surprise, John,
I pray *to* not for you,
think of you not myself,
smile and fall asleep.

Jean Stafford, a Letter

Towmahss Mahnn: that's how you said it . . .
"That's how Mann must say it," I thought.

I can go on imagining you
in your Heidelberry braids and Bavarian
peasant aprons you wore three or four years
after your master's at twenty-one.

How quickly I run through my little set
of favored pictures . . . pictures starved to words.
My memory economizes so prodigally
I know I have suffered theft.

You did miracles I blushed to acknowledge,
outlines for novels more salable than my poems,
my ambiguities lost seven cities down.
Roget's synonyms studded your spoken and written word.

Our days of the great books, scraping and Roman mass—
your confessions had such a vocabulary
you were congratulated by the priests—
I pretended my impatience was concision.

Tortoise and hare
cross the same finishing line—
we learn the spirit is very willing to give up,
but the body is not weak and will not die.

You have spoken so many words and well,
being a woman and you . . . someone must still hear
whatever I have forgotten
or never heard, being a man.

Since 1939

We missed the declaration of war,
we were on our honeymoon train west;
we leafed through the revolutionary thirties'
Poems of Auden, till our heads fell down
swaying with the comfortable
ungainly gait of obsolescence . . .
I miss more things now,
am more consciously mistaken.
I see another girl reading Auden's last book.
She must be very modern,
she dissects him in the past tense.

He is historical now as Munich,
and grew perhaps
to love the rot of capitalism.

We still live
with the devil of his derelictions
he wished to disdain
in the mischievous eccentricity of age.

In our unfinished revolutionary now,
everything seems to end and nothing to begin . . .
The Devil has survived his hollow obits,
and hobbles cursing to his demolition,
a moral heaviness no scales can weigh—
a regurgitation like spots
of yellow buttercups . . .

England like America has lasted
long enough to fear its past,
the habits squashed like wax,
the gay, the prosperous,
their acid of outrage . . .

A decade or so ago,
cavalier African blacks piled
their small English cemetery and dump
to suffocation with statues,
Victorias, Kitcheners, Belfast mercenaries
drained white by rule and carved in soap . . .
caught by the marked cards that earned their keep—
the sovereign misfortune to surpass.

Did they put on too much color like a great actress
for the fulfillment of the dress rehearsal . . .
Did they think they still lived,
if their spirit carried on?

We feel the machine slipping from our hands,
as if someone else were steering;
if we see a light at the end of the tunnel,
it's the light of an oncoming train.

Square of Black

On this book, large enough to write on,
is a sad, black, actual photograph
of Abraham Lincoln and Tad in 1861,
father and son,
their almost matching silver watchchains,
as they stare into the blank ledger,
its murders and failures . . . they.
Old Abe, and old at 52—
in life, in office, no lurking illusion,
clad for the moment in robes of splendor,
passed him unchallenged . . .
Only in a dream was he able to hear,
his voice in the East Room of the White House
saying over his own dead body:
"Lincoln is dead."

Dreams, they've had their vogue,
so alike in their modernist invention,
so dangerously distracted by commonplace,
their literal insistence on the letter,
trivia indistinguishable from tragedy—
his monstrous melodrama terminating
at a playhouse . . . dreaming, overhearing
his own voice,
the colloquial sibilance of the circuit-court,
once freedom, the law and home to Lincoln—
shot while sleeping through the final act.

Fortunately
I only dream inconsequence.
Last night I saw a little
flapping square of pure black cloth.
It flew to the corners of my bedroom,
hugging, fluttering there coquettishly—

a bat, if wing and pelt could be one-color black.
It was a mouse. (So my dream explained.)
It taught me to feed and tame it
with nagging love . . . only existing
in my short dream's immeasurable leisure.

Fetus

(*Front-page picture*, Boston Globe, *February 1975*)

The convicted abortion-surgeon
and his Harvard lawyers are Big League,
altruistic, unpopular men lost in the clouds
above the *friendly* municipal court.
The long severe tiers of windows
are one smear of sunlight multiplied;
the new yellow brick has a cutting edge.

"The law is a sledgehammer,
not a scalpel."

The court cannot reform the misstep
of the motionless moment . . .
So many killers are cleared of killing,
yet we are shocked a fetus can be murdered—
its translucence looms to attention
in bilious X-ray
too young to be strengthened
by our old New England hope of heaven
made unsentimental by our certainty in hell.

Our germ—
no number in the debtbook
to say it lived
once unembarrassed by the flesh.

When the black arrow arrives on the silver tray,
the fetus has no past,
not even an immovable wall of paintings—
no room to stir its thoughts,
no breathless servility
overacting the last day,

writing like a worm
under the contradicting rays of science—
no scared eye on the audience.

Wrap me close, but not too close—
when we wake to our unacceptable age,
will we find our hearts enlarged
and wish all men our brothers—
hypocrites pretending to answer
what we cannot hear?

How much we carry away with us
before dying,
learning we have nothing to take,
like the fetus, the homunculus,
already at four months one pound,
with shifty thumb in mouth—

Our little model . . .

As I drive on, I lift my eyes;
the focus is spidered
with black winter branches
and blackened concrete stores
bonneted for Easter with billboards . . .
Boston snow contracting
like a yellow surgical bandage—
the slut of struggle.
The girl high on the billboard
was ten years my senior in life;
she would have teased my father—
unkillable, unlaid,
disused as the adolescent tan on my hand.
She is a model, and cannot lose her looks,
born a decade too soon for any buyer.

Art of the Possible

"Your profession of making what can't be done
the one thing you can do . . ."

In my parents' townhouse,
a small skylight-covered courtyard,
six feet by nine,
lit two floors of bathrooms—
their wanton windows clear glass above,
and modestly glazed below.
There for a winter or so,
when eleven or twelve,
one year short
of the catastrophic brink of adolescence,
I nightly enjoyed my mother bathing—
not lust, but the lust of the eye.

We sit drinking and forking clams,
a man and a woman three years younger,
table companions for twenty years,
raking over the roster of our acquaintance—
grateful our student euphemisms hide
our trembling hands afraid to lift a fork in public.
"Father Freud brainwashed you to hate your mother."
We stand to leave,
your breasts touch my chest;
under our clothes, our bodies
are but as bodies are.
On the thin ice of our hard age
malignant with surprises,
everything inside us stings, yet chills
knowing the affliction of seduction . . .
Tomorrow
the unbecoming oneness of our ravished body
melts in the light of day.

No engagement, I go . . .
darkness straightens the limping hand,
insomnia finds a hundred justifications
for the inexcusable phrase.
After many lives in marriage,
bedrooms blood-temperature,
my joy in making this room arctic—
a solitary barrenness
finds the cold spots in the bed,
and cherishes their expiring chill.

In the Ward

[FOR ISRAEL CITKOVITZ]

Ten years older in an hour—

I see your face smile,
your mouth is stepped on without bruising.
You are very frightened by the ward,
your companions are chosen for age;
you are the youngest
and sham-flirt with your nurse—
your chief thought is scheming
the elaborate surprise of your escape.

Being old in good times is worse
than being young in the worst.

Five days
on this grill, this mattress
over nothing—
the wisdom of this sickness
is piously physical,
ripping up memory
to find your future—
old beauties, old masters
hoping to lose their minds before they lose their friends.

Your days are dark,
your nights imaginary—
the child says,
heaven is a big house
with lots of water and flowers—
you go in in a trunk.

Your feet are wired above your head.

If you could hear the glaring lightbulb
sing
your old modernist classics—
they are for a lost audience.

Last year
in buoyant unrest,
you gathered two or three young friends
in the *champagne room*
of your coldwater flat,
to explore the precision
and daimonic lawlessness
of Arnold Schönberg born
when music was still imperfect science—
Music,
its ever retreating borderlines of being,
as treacherous, perhaps, to systems,
to fecundity,
as to silence.

*Die Sprache ist unverstanden
doch nicht unverständlich?*

If you keep cutting your losses,
you have no loss to cut.

Nothing you see now
can mean anything;
your will is fixed on the lightbulb,
its blinding impassivity
withholding disquiet,
the art of the possible
that art abhors.

It's an illusion death or technique
can wring the truth from us like water.

What helpless paperishness,
if vocation
is only shouting what we will.

Somewhere your spirit
led the highest life;
all places matched
with that place
come to nothing.

Burial

[FOR ————]

Six or seven swallows drag the air,
their fast play of flight unbroken
as if called by a voice—
the flies become fewer about my head.

A longwinded wasp stumbles on me,
marauding, providing, as if about to sting—
patting, smelling me, caught
in the carnivorous harmony of nature.

The small girl has set a jagged chip
of sandstone on the grave of a crow,
chalked with white Gothic like a valentine:
"For Charlie who died last night."

Your father died last month,
he is buried . . . not too deep to lie
alive like a feather
on the top of the mind.

Ear of Corn

At the head of his table
the wine baron
looks like the old Stravinsky.

There's green on the bread;
all the beautiful girls he knew
are old maids or dead.

One must admire him,
so assured of his triumphant return,
of making it abundantly,
yet spoiling his hopeless odds by talking.

He is drunk on his own wine,
his hundreds of servants filling 14 glasses
in chronological vintage at each place
with incantations of the price.
"It's a sacrilege for *me* to say it . . .
they mustn't hear me . . .
the best drink is a rum-banana daiquiri!"

He is not lacking in love,
someone's young wife is on his right—
"Have you ever returned to a childhood house,
and found it unchanged?
It makes one so angry . . . it's so shrunk,
one wishes it wiped out—if it *is* wiped out,
that, of course, is another kind of catastrophe."

The girl hears and feels maternal.
His eyes never leave her lips.
She cannot cure his hallucination
he can bribe or stare
any woman he wants into orgasm . . .
He fills her ear
with his old sexual gramophone.

Like belief,
he makes nothing happen.

He, she, or she or she—
she is a stream,
one of the bubbles . . . one of the sparks
that flashed from the miscellaneous dish he gobbled.

Her face is delicate and disgusted,
as if she had been robbed, raped,
or repudiated by her mother—
a discarded ear of corn
lying in a sink,
leaf and cornsilk flipped to show
the golden kernels are browned . . .
his first image of a girl who refused.

His great lethargy calms him:
hypnos kai hydor,
Scotch and water—
he no longer asks for love.

Is this the substance hoped for,
after a grasshopper life of profit—
to stand shaking on fine green legs,
to meet the second overflowing of Eros,
himself younger in each young face;
and see in that mirror
a water without the life of water,
a face aging
to less generosity than it had?

Off Central Park

[FOR E.H.]

Here indeed, here for a moment,
here ended—that's new.

Another new thing, your single wooden dice,
three feet high,
and marked with squares like a chessboard,
stands laughing at us on the threshold.

Our light intimacy of reference is unbroken.

The old movables keep their places;
they are more confidently out of style
in their unhurried, almost routine decline.

I can give the dates when they entered our lives:

Cousin Belle's half-sofa,
her carrot dangled before famished heirs,
is twenty years lighter.

The small portrait of Cousin Cassie,
corsetted like the Empress Eugénie
and willed to father when I was seven,
is now too young for me to talk to.

In the bookcase, my Catholic theology,
still too high for temptation—
the same radical reviews
where we first broke into print
are still new to us.

Your gilt urchin-faced angels hang like stars
in the cramped bathroom under the stairs—
they see everything that happens there.

Fast and fallen New York—as if I were home,
I go to the bureau for fresh shirts;
the drawers have the solidity of Spanish kings,
observers of successive peaks of decadence,
set on racks in identical bass-viol coffins—
but only a breath, yours, holds anything together,
a once superfluous, now supernatural, spirit,
the thread and sentence of life we mended 50 times.

Our old world . . . nine-tenths invisible—
here we made over what we were before we met . . .

Outside,
I pass Harriet's subteenager playground,
half-modernized,
then interrupted, as if by a stroke of senility.

The sun of comfort shines on the artist,
the same Academician from our building . . .
he is repeating his *Mont-Saint-Victoire*—
why should a landscape painter
ever leave Central Park?
his subject lies under his nose . . .
his prison?

"After so much suffering," you said,
"I realize we couldn't have lasted
more than another year or two anyway."

Death of a Critic

Dull, disagreeable and dying,
the old men—
they were setups for my ridicule,
till time, the healer, made me theirs.

In the old New York, we said,
"If life could write,
it would have written like us."
Now the lifefluid goes
from the throwaway lighter,
its crimson, cylindrical, translucent
glow grows pale—
O queen of cities, star of morning.

The age burns in me.

The path is cleared and cleared each year,
each year the brush closes;
nature cooperates with us,
then we cooperate no more.

II

The television's ocean-green square
loved and searched as no human face . . .

In my disconnected room,
I improve talking to myself.
I convalesce. I do not enjoy
polemic with my old students,
and place a board across the arms of my chair
to type out letters
they burn for fear of my germs.

Disciples came like swallows from Brazil,
or airborne book reviews from London.
On sleepless nights, when my tragedy
delights the dawdling dawnbirds, I ask
where are their unannounced, familiar faces
I could not recognize.

The students whose enthusiasm
burned holes in the transitory
have graduated to not having been.
It would never do
to have them come back to life again,
they would have the fool's heartiness of ghosts . . .
without references or royalties,
out of work.

Now that I am three parts iced-over,
I see the rose glow in my heater.
In moments of warmth, I see
the beauty who made summer
Long Island tropical.
From the nineties to Nixon,
the same girl, the same bust,
still consciously unwrinkled.
On my screen,
her unspeakable employer
offers her to me nightly,
as if she were his daughter.

Did their panic make me infallible?
Was my integrity my unique
understanding of everything I damned?

Did the musician, Gesualdo,
murder his wife to inherit
her voice of the nightingale?

My criticism survives its victims
buried in the Little Magazines
that featured us concurrently,
the barracuda and his prey.
My maiden reviews,
once the verbal equivalent of murder,
are now a brief, compact pile,
almost as old as I.
They fall apart sallowing,
their stiff pages
chip like dry leaves
flying the tree that fed them.

Under New York's cellular façades
clothed with vitreous indifference,
I dwindle . . . dynamite no more.

I ask for a natural death,
no teeth on the ground,
no blood about the place . . .
It's not death I fear,
but unspecified, unlimited pain.

Endings

[FOR HARRIET WINSLOW]

The leap from three adjectives to an object
is impossible—

legs purple and white
like purple grapes on marble.

The change was surprising though laughable
in the 24 years since my first childish
visit to you in Washington—
my foot now touched the first rung of the ladder,
the sharpest pencil line,
far from my Potomac School, my ABC's
with Miss Locke and Miss Gay.

Our arms reached out to each other
too full of drinks . . .
You joked of your blackouts,
your abstractions,
comic and monumental
even for Washington.
You woke wondering why
you woke in another room,
you woke close to drowning.
Effects are without cause;
your doctors found nothing.
A month later you were paralyzed
and never unknotted . . .

A small spark tears at my head,
a flirting of light brown specks in the sky,
explosive pinpricks,
an unaccountable lapse of time.

When I close my eyes, the image is too real,
the solid colors and perspective of life . . .
the tree night-silvered above a bay becomes
the great globe itself, an eye deadened to royal blue
and buried in a jacket of oak leaves.

Why plan; when we stop?

The wandering virus never surmounts the cluster
it never joined.

My eyes flicker, the immortal
is scraped unconsenting from the mortal.

Part Three

Day by Day

FOR CAROLINE

The Day

It's amazing
the day is still here
like lightning on an open field,
terra firma and transient
swimming in variation,
fresh as when man first broke
like the crocus all over the earth.

From a train, we saw cows
strung out on a hill
at differing heights,
one sex, one herd,
replicas in hierarchy—
the sun had turned
them noonday bright.

They were child's daubs in a book
I read before I could read.

They fly by like a train window:
flash-in-the-pan moments
of the Great Day,
the *dies illa*,
when we lived momently
together forever
in love with our nature—

as if in the end,
in the marriage with nothingness,
we could ever escape
being absolutely safe.

Domesday Book

Let nothing be done twice—

When Harold fell
with an arrow in his eye at Hastings,
the bastard Conqueror taxed
everything in his Domesday Book:
ox, cow, swine,
the villages and hundreds
his French clerks tore to shreds
and fed
to berserk hawk and baron.
His calculated devastation,
never improvidently
merciful to the helpless,
made anarchy anachronism
and English a speech for serfs.

England/Scotland/Ireland
had better days—
now the elephantiasis of the great house
is smothered in the beauty of its English garden
changed already to a feathery, fertile waste,
lawns drenched with the gold-red sorrel.
The hectic, seeded rose
climbs a neglected gravel drive
cratered to save the children from delivery vans.
The beef-red bricks and sky-gray stones
are buried in the jungle leaf of June—
wildflowers take root in the kitchen garden.

The dower house goes with the house,
the dowager with her pale, white cup of tea
she inspired with brandy.

Lathom House, Middleton Manor,
New Hall, Silverton,
Brickling with its crinkled windows
and rose-pink gables
are converted to surgeries, polytechnics,
cells of the understaffed asylum
crumbling on the heads of the mad.

The country houses that rolled
like railways are now
more stationary than anthills—
their service gone. Will they fall
under the ax of penal taxes
they first existed to enact . . .
too grand for any gallery?
Will the house for pleasure
predecease its predecessor,
the cathedral,
once outshone in art and cost?

Cold chimneystacks and greening statuary
outlive the living garden
parceled to irreversible wilderness
by one untended year—
from something to nothing . . .
like King Charles who lost his head
and shared the luck and strange
fibered Puritan violence
of his antagonist, the Protector,
whose carcass
they drew on a hurdle to Tyburn,
hanged and buried under the gallows.

If they have you by the neck, a rope will be found.

Nulle terre sans seigneur.

The old follies, as usual, never return—
the houses still burn
in the golden lowtide steam of Turner.
Only when we start to go,
do we notice the outrageous phallic flare
of the splash flowers that fascinated children.

The reign of the kingfisher was short.

We Took Our Paradise

We took our paradise here—
how else love?

These three weeks the weather
has accreted reek
like a bathroom mirror:
hills, cows, molehills,
the oceanless inland . . .

the harvest
we whistle from grass.

The struck oak that lost
a limb that weighed a ton
still shakes green leaves
and takes the daylight,
as if alive.

Can one bear it; in nature
from seed to chaff no tragedy?

Folly comes from something—
the present, yes,
we are in it;
it's the infection
of things gone . . .

the Atlantic rattling paper
I haven't heard three years.

Why does a man love a woman
more than women?

Lives

Summer is like Hope
to engrave free verse on bronze—
in this room,
the air is blocked by its walls;
I cannot walk to old friends,
as if there were doors.

In the end,
in tagging distance,
I am afraid of falling back,
becoming a child according to the Gospel,
acting with more demand
than I was able to full flower—
in sum
the Great Cycle is the ponderous strum
of this final year.

How could you love, and you so young?

My unhealthy generation—
their lives never stopped stopping,
with ursine step,
one foot bleeding,
without a crutch—
snapdragons,
half-amiable and gallant . . .

their week was so short
they could see it move.

Yet I take joy in remembering the pains
we took to give the ringing statement—
the calendared slip of the scissors
was only poisonous in thought.

It would take a tree-surgeon
to know the blond-faced wheat
and comfortable fleshed-out trees
are crumbling to sawdust.

This August is like a woman
who gets men without moving.

The Spell

Sometimes I begin to fear a dead
lost spirit who claimed he could haunt—
perhaps he could hex me . . . only by haunting himself.
What help were his sermons,
his genius for unrhetorical wit,
his metaphysical grandiosity,
or the hard antisocial ritual he laid on himself,
like a snail's shell to be at home anywhere
and always comfortably himself?
Age came, and then infirmity,
a boyish precocity eagerly willing
to take a joke or two and quote a hundred.
He was not ruled by measure,
or comfortably himself,
when he made
his verse the echo of his conscious mind.
Or when at appointed hours,
he brightly hectored the visitors
in his lodgings, that clean cliff of books
above a wash of trash.
We almost expected a miracle,
when on good days at the dot of six
he changed
his room-chilled black coffee
to spirits in our bitter mugs.
He once changed English to his own demotic.
He was more madly, innocently, at home
on bachelor afternoons,
when he cut short the cocktail hour,
expelled his guests,
and sat down in the ebbing twilight
to the early supper of a child . . .
an old choirboy chirping in his stall,
too tipsy to manage his knife,

free to drink or not to drink . . .
Comme le bon dieu le veut, le temps s'envole.
He was not my double, and haunts me.
He died
generously drinking, too disciplined for a friend.

This Golden Summer

This golden summer,
this bountiful drought,
this crusting bread—
nothing in it is gold.

Its fields have the yellow-white hair
of Patriarchs who lived
on two goats and no tomorrow—
a fertility too rich to breathe.

Our cat, a new mother, put a paw
under my foot, as I held a tray;
her face went white, she streaked screaming
through an open window, an affronted woman.

Is our little season of being together
so unprecarious, I must imagine
the shadow around the corner . . .
downstairs . . . behind the door?

I see even in golden summer
the wilted blowbell spiders
ruffling up impossible angers,
as they shake threads to the light.

We have plucked the illicit corn,
seen the Scriptural
fragility of flowers—
where is our pastoral adolescence?

I will leave earth
with my shoes tied,
as if the walk
could cut bare feet.

Milgate

Yearly, connubial swallows nest
in the sky-flung gutter and stop its mouth.
It is a natural life. Nettles
subdue the fugitive violet's bed,
a border of thistles hedges the drive;
children dart like minnows. They dangle
over the warm, reedy troutbrook.

It's a crime
to get too little from too much.

In mirage, meadow turns to lawn,
in the dredged cowpond, weed is water,
half-naked children beautify,
feud and frighten the squabbling ducks—
from vacation to vacation,
they broaden out to girls, young ladies,
a nightlife on two telephones.

The elderflower is champagne.

Age goes less noticed in humbler life—
the cedar of Lebanon dumbly waves
one defoliated millennial stump;
the yew row, planted under Cromwell
with faith and burnish, keeps its ranks,
unpierceably stolid, young, at ease.

August flames in the rusty sorrel,
a bantam hen hatches wild pheasant chicks,
the dog licks ice cream from a cone;
but mostly the cropped, green, sold-off pastures
give grace to the house, to *Milgate Park*,
its name and service once one in Bearsted,

till uselessness brought privacy,
splendor, extravagance, makeshift
offered at auction for its bricks—
yet for a moment saved by you,
and kept alive another decade,
by your absentminded love,
your lapwing's instinctive elegance,
the glue of your obdurate Ulster will—
Milgate,
enclosures to sun and space to cool,
one mural varied in fifty windows,
sublime and cozy, stripped of creeper,
its severity a blaze of salmon-pink,
its long year altered by our small . . .
easy to run as things made to run.

Realities

Who knows if the live season
will add tomorrow to today?

Young we identified
the sounds of the summer night,
the mating birds,
roadsters and sex
of the incumbent generation.

How little we cost then—
and so many submitted to pain,
and even joy, to bring us here—
they now solid
because we are solid,
we their only outcome.

Their faces, no longer faces, adorn
the golden age of photographs—
thinking, like us, their autumn
the autumn of the world.

Houses grew with them,
increasing like the great conch's
roselipped, steepled shell—
left calcifying in gardens,
where their children multiplied . . .
I cannot believe myself them,
my children more skeptical than I,
misunderstanding those who misunderstood—
hanging on to power by a fingernail.

If I could go through it all again,
the slender iron rungs of growing up,
I would be as young as any,
a child lost
in unreality and loud music.

Ants

Ants
are not under anathema to make it new—
they are too small and penny-proud
to harm us much or hold the human eye
looking downward on them,
like a Goth watching a game of chess.

On this tenth hot day,
the best of a drought summer,
the unthinking insects
leave their heated hills:
warrior, honey-cow and slave.
The earth is rock;
the ants waver
with thread antennae
emptily . . . as if one tactic
did for feeding or seeking
barren fields for drill.

Ants are amazing but not exemplary;
their beehive hurry excludes romance.

Once in time out of mind,
on such a warm day as this,
the ant-heads must have swarmed beyond
the illusive shimmer of the ant-hill,
and crowned slavery with socialism.
They invented the state before and after
Plato's grim arithmetic—a state
unchanging, limited, beyond our reach,
decadence, or denial . . .
their *semper eadem* of good fortune.
Yet not always the same;
the ants repair it yearly,

like the Chinese traditional painter
renewing his repertory flowers—
each touch a stroke for tradition.

They are the lost case of the mind.

I lie staring under an old oak,
stubby, homely, catacombed by ants,
more of a mop than a tree.
I fear the clumsy boughs will fall.
Is its weak, wooden heart strong enough
to bear my weight if I should climb
from knob to knob to the top?
How uneasily I am myself,
as a child I found the sky too close.
Why am I childish now and ask
for daffy days when I tried to read
Walden's ant-war aloud to you for love?

Sheridan

Another day of standstill heat,
old American summer, Old Glory,
only the squeaking, floppy lapwings
and garrulous foreign colony of jackdaws
are English, all else is American.
Placed chestnut trees flower mid-cowfield,
even in harvest time, they swear,
"We always had leaves and ever shall."

Sheridan, you gleam and stall in the heat,
mislaying as many things as people;
your whole plastic armory, claymore,
Nazi helmet, batwings, is lost.
But who would hide weapons that do
everything true weapons should, but hurt?
"You're Mr. Loser," you say, "you lost our guns."
You say it in Kentish cockney: *weir* guns.

How unretentive we become,
yet weirdly naked like you. Today
only the eternal midday separates
you from our unchangeably sunset
and liver-invigorated faces. High-hung,
the period scythe silvers in the sun,
a cutting edge, a bounding line,
between the child's world and the earth—

Our early discovery that only children grow.

Marriage

I

We were middle-class and verismo
enough to suit Van Eyck,
when we crowded together in Maidstone,
patriarch and young wife
with our three small girls
to pose in Sunday-best.
The shapeless comfort of your flowered frock
was transparent against the light,
but the formal family photograph in color
shows only a rousing brawn of shoulder
to tell us you were pregnant.

Even there, Sheridan, though unborn,
was a center of symmetry;
even then he was growing in hiding
toward gaucheness and muscle—
to be a war-
chronicler of vast inaccurate memory.
Later, his weird humor
made him elf and dustman,
like him, early risers.
This summer, he is a soldier—
unlike father or mother,
or anyone he knows,
he can choose both sides:
Redcoat, Minuteman, or George the Third . . .
the ambivalence of the Revolution that made him
half-British, half-American.

II

I turn to the *Arnolfini Marriage*,
and see
Van Eyck's young Italian merchant

was neither soldier nor priest.
In an age of Faith,
he is not abashed to stand weaponless,
long-faced and dwindling
in his bridal bedroom.
Half-Jewish, perhaps,
he is freshly married,
and exiled for his profit to Bruges.
His wife's with child;
he lifts a hand,
thin and white as his face
held up like a candle to bless her . . .
smiling, swelling, blossoming . . .

Giovanni and Giovanna—
even in an age of costumes,
they seem to flash their fineness . . .
better dressed than kings.

The picture is too much like their life—
a crisscross, too many petty facts,
this bedroom
with one candle still burning in the candelabrum,
and peaches blushing on the windowsill,
Giovanni's high-heeled raw wooden slippers
thrown on the floor by her smaller ones . . .
dyed *sang de boeuf*
to match the restless marital canopy.

They are rivals in homeliness and love;
her hand lies like china in his,
her other hand
is in touch with the head of her unborn child.
They wait and pray,
as if the airs of heaven
that blew on them when they married

were now a common visitation,
not a miracle of lighting
for the photographer's sacramental instant.

Giovanni and Giovanna,
who will outlive him by 20 years . . .

The Withdrawal

I

Only today and just for this minute,
when the sunslant finds its true angle,
you can see yellow and pinkish leaves spangle
our gentle, fluffy tree—
suddenly the green summer is momentary . . .
Autumn is my favorite season—
why does it change clothes and withdraw?

This week the house went on the market—
suddenly I wake among strangers;
when I go into a room, it moves
with embarrassment, and joins another room.

I don't need conversation, but you to laugh with—
you and a room and a fire,
cold starlight blowing through an open window—
whither?

II

After sunfall, heaven is melodramatic,
a temporary, puckering, burning green.
The patched-up oak
and blacker, indelible pines
have the indigestible meagerness of spines.

One wishes heaven had less solemnity:
a sensual table
with five half-filled bottles of red wine
set round the hectic carved roast—
Bohemia for ourselves
and the familiars of a lifetime
charmed to communion by resurrection—
running together in the rain to mail a single letter,
not the chafe and cling
of this despondent chaff.

III

Yet for a moment, the children
could play truant from their tuition.

IV

When I look back, I see a collapsing
accordion of my receding houses,
and myself receding
to a boy of twenty-five or thirty,
too shopworn for less, too impressionable for more—
blackmaned, illmade
in a washed blue workshirt and coalblack trousers,
moving from house to house,
still seeking a boy's license
to see the countryside without arrival.

Hell?

Darling,
terror in happiness may not cure the hungry future,
the time when any illness is chronic,
and the years of discretion are spent on complaint—

until the wristwatch is taken from the wrist.

Logan Airport, Boston

Your blouse,
Concord grapes on white,
a souvenir you snatched at the airport,
shone blindingly up the gangway
to a sky overcrowded at rush-hour.
Below the flying traffic,
thin, dwindling yellow trees were feverish,
as if frightened
by your limitless prospect on the blue.

I see you, you are hardly there—
it's as though I watched a painter
do sketches of your head
that by some consuming fire
erased themselves,
until I stared at a blank sheet.

Now in the brown air of our rental,
I need electricity even on fair days,
as I decamp from window to window
to catch the sun.
I am blind with seeing;
the toys you brought home like groceries
firetrap on the stairs.

Is it cynical to deliquesce,
as Adam did in age,
though outwardly goldleaf,
true metal, and make-up?

Our mannerisms harden—
a bruise is immortal,
the instant egg on my shin
I got from braking a car
too sharply a year ago
stays firm brown and yellow,
the all-weather color for death.

I cannot bring back youth with a snap of my belt,
I cannot touch you—
your absence is presence,
the undrinkable blaze
of the sun on both shores of the airport.

Bright sun of my bright day,
I thank God for being alive—
a way of writing I once thought heartless.

Wellesley Free

(A reading)

I

The new blower machine
puffs lost leaves from the yard
with a muffled clang—
whirs my head like the barber,
when my hair was short enough to cut.
The best machine can be wrecked

at 56.
I balance on my imbalance,
and count the black and white steps
to my single room.
Space is mere clearance
since you flew to Europe.

Our boys' school train would pass Wellesley
without slowing. We weren't free.

The girls go airily into the night;
boys are temporary
and rev their cars
and cough out the midnight bells
and leave the College for Women
lighter without men.

II

I have fallen from heaven.
In my overnight room,
3 French windows to the right,
and 3 to the left
cast bright oblique reflections
unnerving with their sparkle.

Coleridge,
the author of *Dejection*,
thought
genius is the discovery
of subjects remote
from my life.

I cannot read.
Everything I've written
is greenish brown,
as if the words
refused to sound.
A lemon-squeezer night—

I cannot sleep solo,
I loathe age with terror,
and will be that . . .
eat the courage of my selfishness
unredeemed by the student's
questionmark potential . . .

70° outside,
and almost December.

To Mother

I've come a third time
to live in your dour, luxurious Boston;
I almost lifted the telephone to dial you,
forgetting you have no dial.
Your exaggerating humor,
the opposite of deadpan,
the opposite of funny to a son,
is mine now—
your bolting blood, your lifewanting face,
the unwilled ruffle of drama in your voice.

You were
Josephine Beauharnais, la femme militaire.

The humpback brick sidewalks of Harvard
kick me briskly,
as if allowed the license of age;
persons who could hardly walk or swallow,
when I was a student,
angrily grate like old squirrels
with bandages of white hair about their ears.
I see myself change in my changed friends—
may I live longer, yet break no record.

Becoming ourselves,
we lose our nerve for children.

One crummy plant can inspire a whole room—
yours were not crummy—bulb, sheath, seductive stem,
the lily that lifts its flag a moment
puckering on the white pebbles of a whiter pot.
Your parlor was a reproach. I wish I were there with you,
the minutes not counted, but not forever—

you used to brush mantelpiece and banister
with the forefinger of a fresh white glove for dust.

"Why do we keep expecting life to be easy,
when we know it never can be?"

I enjoyed hearing scandal on you. Much came
from others, your high-school friends, themselves now dust.
It has taken me the time since you died
to discover you are as human as I am . . .
if I am.

Robert T. S. Lowell

Son

I futilely wished
to meet you at my age;
the date never came off.
It would take two lifetimes
to pick the crust
and uncover the face
under our two menacing,
iconoclastic masks.

Father

You had your chance to meet me.
My father died before I was born.
I was half orphaned . . . such a son
as the stork seldom flings to ambition.

I lay
in the lee of my terrible elders;
the age had a largeness I lacked,
an appetite that forgave everything . . .
our Spanish War's oversubscribed,
battle-bright decks.

At fourteen
I enlisted at Annapolis.

At twenty-seven
I proposed in uniform
and married your mother—
a service I served with even wistfulness,
enslaved by the fire I courted.

I only wished idly
with dilated eyes
to relive my life.

Your game-leg beagle would tiptoe to my room,
if she heard you were asleep—
loneliness to loneliness!

You think that having
your two children on the same floor this fall,
one questioning, one climbing and breaking,
is like living on a drum
or a warship—it can't be that,
it's your life, and dated like mine.

For Sheridan

We only live between
before we are and what we were.

In the lost negative
you exist,
a smile, a cypher,
an old-fashioned face
in an old-fashioned hat.

Three ages in a flash:
the same child in the same picture,
he, I, you,
chockablock, one stamp
like mother's wedding silver—

gnome, fish, brute cherubic force.

We could see clearly
and all the same things
before the glass was hurt.

Past fifty, we learn with surprise and a sense
of suicidal absolution
that what we intended and failed
could never have happened—
and must be done better.

Bright Day in Boston

Joy of standing up my dentist,
my X-ray plates like a broken Acropolis . . .

Joy to idle through Boston,
my head full of young Henry Adams
and his unnoticed white silk armband,
worn for a day to free the slaves.

An epoch ago the instant
when one could live anywhere
unendangered, unendangering
anything but respect . . .

Impregnable and out of place
on the sunny side of the old Mall,
now housing for students—
their blouses coquetting in the purple glass
of the great bastion-bayed mansion
of Augustus Lowell,
martinet of his mills and lover of roses . . .

No one has troubled to file away
the twisted black iron window-bars,
their taunt of dead craft.

For no reason, the slender streetlamps,
of identical delicate iron
and weak as candles,
flicker all day.

In a city of murder, an American city.

This house, that house—
I have lived in them all,
straight brick without figure.

My fluids command my heart
to go out to the loser—always;
but it is murder to pity the rich,
even when they are as gone
as Hector, tamer of horses—
always doomed to return,
to be with us always like the poor.

Grass Fires

In the realistic memory
the memorable must be forgone;
it never matters,
except in front of our eyes.

I made it a warning,
a cure, that stabilized nothing.
We cannot recast the faulty drama,
play the child,
unable to align
his toppling, elephantine script,
the hieroglyphic letters
he sent home.

I hold big kitchen matches to flaps of frozen grass
to smoke a rabbit from its hole—
then the wind bites them, then they catch,
the grass catches, fire everywhere,
everywhere
inextinguishable roots,
the tree grandfather planted for his shade,
combusting, towering
over the house he anachronized with stone.

I can't tell you how much larger
and more important it was than I,
how many summers before conscience
I enjoyed it.

My grandfather towered above me,
"You damned little fool,"
nothing to quote, but for him original.
The fire-engines deployed with stage bravado,
yet it was I put out the fire,

who slapped it to death with my scarred leather jacket.
I snuffed out the inextinguishable root,
I—
really I can do little,
as little now as then,
about the infernal fires—
I cannot blow out a match.

Phillips House Revisited

A weak clamor like ice giving . . .

Something sinister and comforting
in this return after forty years' arrears
to death and Phillips House . . .
this irreverent absence of pain,
less than the ordinary that daily irks—
except I cannot entirely get my breath,
as if I were muffled in snow,
our winter's inverted gray sky
of frozen slush,
its usual luminous lack of warmth.

This room was brighter then
when grandfather filled it,
brilliant for his occasion
with his tallness, reddish tan and pain.

Twice he was slipped
champagne and oysters
by a wild henna-dyed niece by marriage
he had promised to cut.

This seemed good to him and us.

He could still magnetize the adolescent.

I too am passed my half-bottle . . .
no oyster.

But these forty years grandfather would insist
have turned the world on its head—
their point was
to extinguish him like a stranded crab.

He needed more to live than I,
his foot could catch hold anywhere
and dynamite his way to the gold again—
for the world is generous to the opportune,
its constantly self-renewing teams of favorites.

St. Mark's, 1933

The fourth form dining-table
was twenty feet by four,
six boys to a side;
at one end, Mr. Prendie the Woodchuck,
dead to the world, off picking daisies;
at the other end, another boy.
Mid-meal, they began
to pull me apart.
"Why is he always grubbing in his nose?"
"Because his nose is always snotty."
"He likes to wipe his thumb in it."
"Cal's a creep of the first water."
"He had a hard-on for his first shower."
"He only presses his trousers once a term."
"Every other term." "No term."
Over the years I've lost
the surprise and sparkle of that slang
our abuse made perfect.
"Dimbulb." "Fogbound." "Droopydrawers."
"The man from the Middle West."
"Cal is a slurp."
"A slurp farts in the bathtub."
"So he can bite the bubbles."
How did they say my face
was pearl-gray like toe-jam—
that I was foul
as the gymsocks I wore a week?
A boy next to me breathed my shoes,
and lay choking on the bench.

"Cal doesn't like everyone."
"Everyone doesn't like Cal."
"Cal,
who is your best friend at this table?"
"Low-ell, Low-ell"
(to the tune of *Noël, Noël*).

This was it, though I bowdlerize . . .
All term I had singled out classmates,
and made them listen to and remember
the imperfections of their friends.
I broke one on the other—
but who could break them,
they were so many,
rich, smooth and loved?

I was fifteen;
they made me cry in public.
Chicken?

Perhaps they had reason . . .
even now
my callous unconscious drives me
to torture my closest friend.

Huic ergo parce, Deus.

To Frank Parker

Forty years ago we were here
where we are now,
the same erotic May-wind blew
the trees from there to here—

the same tang of metal in the mouth,
the dirt-pierced wood of Cambridge.

Sometimes
you are so much younger than your face,
I know I am seeing your old face—
the hampered Henry James
mockery of your stutter,
your daily fear of choking, dying—
in school, loudness not words
gave character to the popular boy's voice.

We looked in the face of the other
for what we were.
Once in the common record heat
of June in Massachusetts,
we sat by the school pool
talking out the soul-lit night
and listened to the annual
unsuffering voice of the tree frogs,
green, aimless and wakened:
"I want to write." "I want to paint."

Was it I wanted you to paint? . . .

Age is another species,
the nothing-voiced. The very old
made grandfather look vulgarly young,
when he drove me to feed them at their home.

We will have their thoughtful look,
as if uncertain
who had led our lives.

The past changes more than the present.

Wherever there's grass, there is pollen,
the asthma of high summer—
the inclination to drink, not eat . . .

"Let us go into the garden,
or shall I say the yard?"
Why have you said this twice, Frank?
The garden has no flowers,
or choice of color,
the thick wet clump of grass
thins to red clay,
like an Indian's shaved and tufted head,
or yours—
we once claimed alliance with the Redskin.
What is won by surviving,
if two glasses of red wine are poison?

Morning after Dining with a Friend

(Some weeks after Logan Airport)

Waking wifeless is now a habit—
hearing the human-abstract rush of traffic,
another night, another day
entertaining nothing but my thoughts—

Why have I twisted your kind words
and tortured myself till morning?

My brain keeps flashing back last night—
a booth in the Greek restaurant,
now fronting the Boston Combat Zone—
"We'd be mad not to take a taxi back."

"I think Frost liked me better
but found you more amusing."

I met you first at the old Met Opera Club,
shy, correct, in uniform,
your regulation on active duty
substitute for black-tie—

Poet and aviator
at 36,
the eternal autumn of youth.

That image has gained body;
yet shrinks back this morning
to its greener Platonic shade,
the man of iron—

not drinking, terrified
of losing your mind . . .
turning to me, calm
by a triumph of impersonation:

"If you could come a little nearer
the language of the tribe."

Return in March

Tannish buds and green buds,
hidden yesterday, pioneers today.
The Georgian thirties' Harvard houses
have shed their brashness in forty years;
architecture suffers decline with dignity
and requisitions its atmosphere—
our hope is in things that spring.

Tonight in the middle of melting Boston,
a brick chimney tapers, and points a ladder
of white smoke into the blue-black sky.

Suburban Surf

(After Caroline's return)

You lie in my insomniac arms,
as if you drank sleep like coffee.

Then,
like a bear tipping a hive for honey,
you shake the pillow for French cigarettes.

No conversation—
then suddenly as always cars
helter-skelter for feed like cows—

suburban surf come alive,

diamond-faceted like your eyes,
glassy, staring lights
lighting the way they cannot see—

friction, constriction etc.
the racket killing
gas like alcohol.

Long, unequal whooshing waves
break in volume,
always very loud enough to hear—

méchants, mechanical—

soothe, delay, divert
the crescendo always surprisingly attained
in a panic of breathlessness—

too much assertion and skipping
of the heart to greet the day . . .
the truce with uncertain heaven.

A false calm is the best calm.

In noonday light,
the cars are tin, stereotype and bright,
a farce
of their former selves at night—
invisible as exhaust,
personal as animals.

Gone
the sweet agitation of the breath of Pan.

III

Turtle

I pray for memory—
an old turtle,
absentminded, inelastic,
kept afloat by losing touch . . .
no longer able to hiss or lift
a useless shield against the killer.

Turtles age, but wade out amorously,
half-frozen fossils, yet knight-errant
in a foolsdream of armor.
The smaller ones climb rocks to broil in comfort.

Snapping turtles only submerge.
They have survived . . . not by man's philanthropy.

I hunted them in school vacations.
I trampled an acre of driftstraw
floating off the muskrats' loose nests.
Here and there, a solitary turtle
craned its brown Franciscan cowl
from one of twenty waterholes.
In that brew, I stepped
on a turtle's smooth, invisible back.
It was like escaping quicksand.
I drew it in my arms by what I thought was tail—
a tail? I held a foreleg.
I could have lost a finger.

This morning when
the double-brightness of the winter sun
wakes me from the film of dreaming,
my bedroom is unfamiliar. I see

three snapping turtles squatted on my drifting clothes—
two rough black logs . . . the third is a nuzzler
dressed in see-through yellow tortoiseshell,
a puppy squeaking and tweaking
my empty shirt for milk.

They are stale and panting;
what is dead in me wakes their appetite.
When they breathe, they seem to crack apart,
crouched motionless on tiptoe
with crooked smiles
and high-school nicknames on their tongues,
as if they wished to relive
the rawness that let us meet as animals.
Nothing has passed between us but time.

"You've wondered where we were these years?
Here are we."

They lie like luggage—
my old friend the turtle . . . Too many pictures
have screamed from the reel . . . in the rerun,
the snapper holds on till sunset—
in the awful instantness of retrospect,
its beak
works me underwater drowning by my neck,
as it claws away pieces of my flesh
to make me small enough to swallow.

Seventh Year

Seven years ago, my instantly dispelled
dream of putting the place on its feet—

never again—I see it clearly,
but with the blind glass eyes of a doll.

This early January
the shallow brown lakes on the drive
already catch
the first spring negative of the birds.

The burnished oxweight cows
now come closer to us and crash
foot over foot through vine and glass—

lowing to one another with the anxious
human voice of a boy calling cows.

We are at least less run-down
than Longfellow's house on Brattle Street,
where only his bearded bust of Zeus,
his schoolday self, is young,

where the long face of his wife
who burned to death
ages as if alive

as Longfellow, whose hand held
the dismissive laurel bough
that hides his grave.

The New England Augustans
lived so long one thought
the snow of their hair would never melt.

Where is Hart Crane,
the disinherited, the fly by night,
who gave
the drunken Dionysus firmer feet?

To each the rotting natural to his age.

Dividing the minute we cannot prolong,
I stand swaying at the end of the party,
a half-filled glass in each hand—
I too swayed
by the hard infatuate wind of love
they cannot hear.

Shaving

Shaving's the one time I see my face,
I see it aslant as a carpenter's problem—
though I have gaunted a little,
always the same face
follows my hand with thirsty eyes.

Never enough hours in a day—
I lie confined and groping,
monomaniacal,
jealous of even a shadow's intrusion—
a nettle
impossible to deflect . . .
unable to follow the drift
of children, their blurting third-degree.

For me,
a stone is as inflammable as a paper match.

The household comes to a stop—
you too, head bent,
inking, crossing out . . . frowning
at times with a face open as a sunflower.

We are lucky to have done things as one.

Runaway

You would sit like a folded beach-chair
in the tallest, hardest armchair . . .
out of character churchly—
or prop your left elbow on a rug
before the soiling fire
that turned your fingernails to coal.
Winterlong
and through the fleeting cool Kentish summer—
obstinately scowling
to focus your hypnotic, farsighted eyes
on a child's pale blue paper exam book—
two dozens . . . carpeting an acre of floor,
while a single paragraph in your large,
looping, legible hand exhausted a whole book.
A born athlete; now a half hour typing
with your uncorrected back
made a week's infection certain.
Out of your wreckage, beauty, wealth,
gallantries, wildness, came your book,
Great Granny Webster's
paralyzing legacy of privation,
her fey Celtic daughter's
death in an asylum,
your Aunt Veronica's manicly gay
youthful, then ultimate, suicide,
your father's betrayal of you,
rushing to his military death in Burma,
annexed for England
by his father's father, the Viceroy . . .
There's so much else—our life.
At the sick times, our slashing,
drastic decisions made us runaways.

Caroline in Sickness

Tonight the full moon is stopped by trees
or the wallpaper between our windows—
on the threshold of pain,
light doesn't exist,
and yet the glow is smarting
enough to read a Bible
to keep awake and awake.
You are very sick,
you remember how the children,
you and your cousin,
Miss Fireworks and Miss Icicle,
first drove alone with learners' cards
in Connemara, and popped a paper bag—
the rock that broke your spine.
Thirty years later, you still suffer
your spine's spasmodic, undercover life . . .
Putting off a luncheon,
you say into the telephone,
"Next month, if I'm still walking."
I move to keep moving;
the cold white wine is dis-spirited—
Moon, stop from dark apprehension . . .
shine as is your custom,
scattering this roughage to find sky.

Stars

Caged in fiction's iron bars,
I give this voice to you
with tragic diction to rebuke the stars—
it isn't you, and yet it's you.

"Will you, like Goethe, fall
to oblivion in my arms;
then talk about the stars?
Say they light militant campfires,
storm heaven while I sleep?
Not now—
my spine is hurting me,
I can only lie face down,
a gross weight innocent—
if you will let me sleep—
of seduction, speech, or pain.
I'm too drugged to do anything,
or help you watch the sky.
I am indifferent to the stars—
their ranks are too docile and mathematical
to regroup if once scattered
like comatose sheep . . .
I am indifferent—
what woman has the measure of a man,
who only has to care about himself
and follow the stars'
extravagant, useless journey across the sky,
to divert me from the absence of the sun?
Because they cannot love, they need no love."

If you heard God is dead,
the old monopolist,
who made us to take us apart—
would you stand upright in spite of your spine?

"I sleep,
an old walnut soaked in rum,
too slippery for the stars to crack
in their rigid, identical glass wheels . . .
If God is dead,
how can I be certain another old man
will drop again from the stars,
from sixty thousand fathoms away,
and halt by the post of my bed—
motionless with ill-omened power?
A new old lover
might hurt a thousand times worse . . .
But my beloved
is godlike, tantalizing,
made in the image of a man
too young to be frightened of women.
He can only appear in all my dreams."

Seesaw

The night dark before its hour—
heavily, steadily,
the rain lashes and sprinkles
to complete its task—
as if assisting
the encroachments of our bodies
we occupy but cannot cure.

Sufferer, how can you help me,
if I use your sickness
to increase my own?

Will we always be
one up, the other down,
one hitting bottom, the other
flying through the trees—
seesaw inseparables?

Ten Minutes

The single sheet keeps shifting on the double bed,
the more I kick it smooth, the less it covers;
it is the bed I made.
Others have destinations, my train is aimless.
I know I will fall off into the siding and thistle—
imagining the truth will hide my lies.

Mother under one of her five-minute spells
had a flair for total recall,
and told me, item by item, person by person,
how my relentless, unpredictable selfishness
had disappointed and removed
anyone who tried to help—
but I cannot correct the delicate compass-needle
so easily set ajar.

I am companionless;
occasionally, I see a late, suicidal headlight
burn on the highway and vanish.
Now the haunted vacancy fills with friends—
they are waspishly familiar and aggrieved,
a rattling makeshift of mislaid faces,
a whiplash of voices. They cry,
"Can you love me, can you love me?
Oh hidden in your bubble and protected by your wife,
and luxuriously nourished without hands,
you wished us dead,
but vampires are too irreplaceable to die."

They stop, as cars that have the greenlight
stop, and let a pedestrian go . . .
Though I work nightshift,
there's no truth in this processing of words—
the dull, instinctive glow inside me
refuels itself, and only blackens
such bits of paper brought to feed it . . .

My frightened arms
anxiously hang out before me like bent L's,
as if I feared I was a laughingstock,
and wished to catch and ward you off . . .
This is becoming a formula:
after the long, dark passage,
I offer you my huddle of flesh and dismay.
"This time it was all night," I say.
You answer, "Poseur,
why, you haven't been awake ten minutes."

.   .   .

I grow too merry,
when I stand in my nakedness to dress.

Visitors

To no good
they enter at angles and on the run—
two black verticals are suddenly four
ambulance drivers in blue serge,
or the police doing double-duty.
They comb our intimate, messy bedroom,
scrutinize worksheets
illegible with second-thoughts,
then shed them in their stride,
as if they owned the room. They do.
They crowd me and scatter—inspecting
my cast-off clothes for clues?
They are fat beyond the call of duty—
with jocose civility,
they laugh at everything I say:
"Yesterday I was thirty-two, a threat
to the establishment because I was young."
The bored woman sergeant
is amused by the tiger-toothed samurai
grinning on a Japanese hanging—
"What would it cost? Where could I buy one?"

I can see through the moonlit dark;
on the grassy London square,
black cows ruminate in uniform,
lowing routinely like a chainsaw.
My visitors are good beef, they too make
one falsely feel the earth is solid,
as they hurry to secretly telephone
from their ambulance. Click, click, click,
goes the red, blue, and white light
burning with aristocratic negligence—
so much busywork.
When they regroup in my room, I know

their eyes have never left their watches.
"Come on, sir." "Easy, sir."
"Dr. Brown will be here in ten minutes, sir."
Instead, a metal chair unfolds into a stretcher.
I lie secured there, but for my skipping mind.
They keep bustling.
"Where you are going, Professor,
you won't need your Dante."
What will I need there?
Is that a handcuff rattling in a pocket?

I follow my own removal,
stiffly, gratefully even, but without feeling.
Why has my talkative
teasing tongue stopped talking?
My detachment must be paid for,
tomorrow will be worse than today,
heaven and hell will be the same—
to wait in foreboding
without the nourishment of drama . . .
assuming, then as now,
this didn't happen to me—
my little strip of eternity.

Three Freuds

By the faint Burne-Jones
entrance window to *The Priory*,
is a bearded marble bust
of dear, dead old Dr. Wood blanche-white,
no name for comedy,
but our founder anticipating me
like an intuitive friend
or doorman in the cold outside his home.
He looks like Sigmund Freud,
too high on bonhomie,
cured by his purgatory of mankind.
Inside the window, is a live patient,
a second bearded Freud,
no Freud, though polished
as the vacant monolith of Dr. Wood . . .
The old boy is not artificial
or disinterested,
yet rudderless and titled,
when he queues at the cold buffet
to pluck up coleslaw in his hands.
When you emerge
it may seem too late.
You chose to go
where you knew I could not follow.

Home

Our ears put us in touch with things unheard of—
the trouble is the patients are tediously themselves,
fussing, confiding . . . committed voluntaries,
immune to the outsider's horror.
The painter who burned both hands
after trying to kill her baby, says,
"Is there no one in Northampton
who goes to the Continent in the winter?"
The alcoholic convert keeps smiling,
"Thank you, Professor, for saving my life;
you taught me homosexuality is a heinous crime."
I hadn't. I am a thorazined fixture
in the immovable square-cushioned chairs
we preoccupy for seconds like migrant birds.

"Remarkable breakdown, remarkable recovery"—
but the breakage can go on repeating
once too often.

*Why is it so hard for them to accept
the very state of happiness is wrong?*

Cups and saucers stamped with the hospital's name
go daily to the tap and are broken.
In the morgue and hospice of the National Museum,
our poor bones and houseware
are lucky to end up in bits and pieces
embalmed between the eternal and tyrants,
their high noses rubbed rough.
How quickly barred-windowed hospitals and museums go—
the final mover has all the leisure in the world.

We have none. Since nature,
our unshakable mother, will grow impatient with us,
we might envy museum pieces
that can be pasted together or disfigured
and feel no panic of indignity.

At visiting hours, you could experience
my sickness only as desertion . . .
Dr. Berners compliments you again,
"A model guest . . . we would welcome
Robert back to Northampton any time,
the place suits him . . . he is so strong."
When you shuttle back chilled to London,
I am on the wrong end of a dividing train—
it is my failure with our fragility.

If he has gone mad with her,
the poor man can't have been very happy,
seeing too much and feeling it
with one skin-layer missing.

       .   .   .

The immovable chairs have swallowed up the patients,
and speak with the eloquence of emptiness.
By each the same morning paper lies unread:
January 10, 1976.
I cannot sit or stand two minutes,
yet walk imagining a dialogue
between the devil and myself,
not knowing which is which or worse,
saying,
as one would instinctively say Hail Mary,
I wish I could die.
Less than ever I expect to be alive
six months from now—
1976,
a date I dare not affix to my grave.

The Queen of Heaven, I miss her,
we were divorced. She never doubted
the divided, stricken soul
could call her Maria,
and rob the devil with a word.

Shadow

I must borrow from Walt Whitman to praise this night,
twice waking me smiling, mysteriously in full health,
twice delicately calling me to the world.
Praise be to sleep and sleep's one god,
the Voyeur, the Mother,
Job's tempestuous, inconstant I AM . . .
who soothes the doubtful murmurs of the heart.

Yet to do nothing up there but adore,
to comprehend nothing but the invisible night—
fortunately the narcoticized
Christian heaven cannot be dreamed or staffed.

If I had a dream of hell
it would be packing up a house
with demons eternally asking
thought-provoking questions.

I have watched the shadow of the crow,
a Roman omen,
cross my shaking hand,
an enigma even for us to read,
a crowsfoot scribble—
when I was with my friend,
I never knew that I had hands.

A man without a wife
is like a turtle without a shell—

this pending hour, this tapeworm minute,
this pending minute, I wait for you to ring—
two in unhealth.

Yet the day is too golden for sleep,
the traffic too sustained . . .
twang-twang of the asylum's leaden bass—
those bleached hierarchies,
moving and shifting like white hospital attendants,
their single errand to reassure the sick.

Notice

The resident doctor said,
"We are not deep in ideas, imagination or enthusiasm—
how can we help you?"
I asked,
"These days of only poems and depression—
what can I do with them?
Will they help me to notice
what I cannot bear to look at?"

The doctor is forgotten now
like a friend's wife's maiden-name.
I am free
to ride elbow to elbow on the rush-hour train
and copy on the back of a letter,
as if alone:
"When the trees close branches and redden,
their winter skeletons are hard to find—"
to know after long rest
and twenty miles of outlying city
that the much-heralded spring is here,
and say,
"Is this what you would call a blossom?"
Then home—I can walk it blindfold.
But we must notice—
we are designed for the moment.

Shifting Colors

I fish until the clouds turn blue,
weary of self-torture, ready to paint
lilacs or confuse a thousand leaves,
as landscapists must.

My eye returns to my double,
an ageless big white horse,
slightly discolored by dirt
cropping the green shelf diagonal
to the artificial troutpond—
unmoving, it shifts as I move,
and works the whole field in the course of the day.

Poor measured, neurotic man—
animals are more instinctive virtuosi.

Ducks splash deceptively like fish;
fish break water with the wings of a bird to escape.

A hissing goose sways in stationary anger;
purple bluebells rise in ledges on the lake.

A single cuckoo gifted with a pregnant word
shifts like the sun from wood to wood.

All day my miscast troutfly buzzes about my ears
and empty mind.

But nature is sundrunk with sex—
how could a man fail to notice, man
the one pornographer among the animals?
I seek leave unimpassioned by my body,
I am too weak to strain to remember, or give
recollection the eye of a microscope. I see

horse and meadow, duck and pond,
universal consolatory
description without significance,
transcribed verbatim by my eye.

This is not the directness that catches
everything on the run and then expires—
I would write only in response to the gods,
like Mallarmé who had the good fortune
to find a style that made writing impossible.

Unwanted

Too late, all shops closed—
I alone here tonight on *Antabuse*,
surrounded only by iced white wine and beer,
like a sailor dying of thirst on the Atlantic—
one sip of alcohol might be death,
death for joy.
Yet in this tempting leisure,
good thoughts drive out bad;
causes for my misadventure, considered
for forty years too obvious to name,
come jumbling out
to give my simple autobiography a plot.

I read an article on a friend,
as if recognizing my obituary:
"Though his mother loved her son consumingly,
she lacked a really affectionate nature;
so he always loved what he missed."
This was John Berryman's mother, not mine.

Alas, I can only tell my own story—
talking to myself, or reading, or writing,
or fearlessly holding back nothing from a friend,
who believes me for a moment
to keep up conversation.

I was surer, wasn't I, once . . .
and had flashes when I first found
a humor for myself in images,
farfetched misalliance
that made evasion a revelation?

Dr. Merrill Moore, the family psychiatrist,
had unpresentable red smudge eyebrows,
and no infirmity for tact—
in his conversation or letters,
each phrase a new
paragraph,
implausible as the million
sonnets he rhymed into his dictaphone,
or dashed on windshield writing-pads,
while waiting out a stoplight—
scattered pearls, some true.
Dead he is still a mystery,
once a crutch to writers in crisis.
I am two-tongued, I will not admit
his Tennessee rattling saved my life.
Did he become mother's lover
and prey
by rescuing her from me?
He was thirteen years her junior . . .
When I was in college, he said, "You know
you were an unwanted child?"
Was he striking my parents to help me?
I shook him off the scent by pretending
anyone is unwanted in a medical sense—
lust our only father . . . and yet
in that world where an only child
was a scandal—
unwanted before I am?

That year Carl Jung said to mother in Zurich,
"If your son is as you have described him,
he is an incurable schizophrenic."

In 1916
father on sea-duty, mother with child
in one house with her affectionate mother-in-law,
unconsuming, already consumptive ...
bromidic to mother ... Mother,
I must not blame you for carrying me in you
on your brisk winter lunges across
the desperate, refusey Staten Island beaches,
their good view skyscrapers on Wall Street ...
for yearning seaward, far from any home, and saying,
"I wish I were dead, I wish I were dead."
Unforgivable for a mother to tell her child—
but you wanted me to share your good fortune,
perhaps, by recapturing the disgust of those walks;
your credulity assumed we survived,
while weaklings fell with the dead and dying.

That consuming love,
woman's everlasting *cri de coeur*,
"When you have a child of your own, you'll know."
Her dowry for her children ...

One thing is certain—compared with my wives,
mother was stupid. Was she?
Some would not have judged so—
among them, her alcoholic patients,
those raconteurish, old Boston young men,
whose fees, late in her life
and to everyone's concern,
she openly halved with Merrill Moore.
Since time out of mind, mother's gay hurting
assessments of enemies and intimates
had made her a formidable character
to her "reading club," seven ladies,
who since her early twenties
met once a week through winters
in their sitting rooms for confidence and tea—

she couldn't read a book . . .
How many of her statements began with,
But Papá always said or *Oh Bobby* . . .
if she Byronized her father and son,
she saw her husband as a valet sees through a master.

She was stupider than my wife . . .
When I was three months,
I rocked back and forth howling
for weeks, for weeks each hour . . .
Then I found the thing I loved most
was the anorexia Christ
swinging on Nellie's gaudy rosary.
It disappeared, I said nothing,
but mother saw me poking strips of paper
down a floor-grate to the central heating.
"Oh Bobby, do you want to set us on fire?"
"Yes . . . that's where Jesus is." I smiled.

Is the one unpardonable sin
our fear of not being wanted?
For this, will mother go on cleaning house
for eternity, and making it unlivable?
Is getting well ever an art,
or art a way to get well?

The Downlook

For the last two minutes, the retiring monarchy
of the full moon looks down on the first chirping sparrows—
nothing lovelier than waking to find
another breathing body in my bed . . .
glowshadow halfcovered with dayclothes like my own,
caught in my arms.

Last summer nothing dared impede
the flow of the body's thousand rivulets of welcome,
winding effortlessly, yet with ambiguous invention—
safety in nearness.

Now the downlook, the downlook—small fuss,
nothing that could earn a line or picture
in the responsible daily paper we'll be reading,
an anthology of the unredeemable world,
beyond the accumulative genius of prose or this—
a day that sharpens apprehension by dulling;
each miss must be a mile,
if one risk the narrow two-lane highway.

It's impotence and impertinence to ask directions,
while staring right and left in two-way traffic.

There's no greater happiness in days of the downlook
than to turn back to recapture former joy.

Ah loved perhaps before I knew you,
others have been lost like this,
yet found foothold
by winning the dolphin from the humming water.

How often have my antics
and insupportable, trespassing tongue
gone astray and led me to prison . . .
to lying . . . kneeling . . . standing.

Thanks-Offering for Recovery

The airy, going house grows small
tonight, and soft enough to be crumpled up
like a handkerchief in my hand.
Here with you by this hotbed of coals,
I am the *homme sensuel*, free
to turn my back on the lamp, and work.
Something has been taken off,
a wooden winter shadow—
goodbye nothing. I give thanks, thanks—
thanks too for this small
Brazilian *ex voto*, this primitive head
sent me across the Atlantic by my friend . . .
a corkweight thing,
to be offered *Deo gratias* in church
on recovering from head-injury or migraine—
now mercifully delivered in my hands,
though shelved awhile unnoticing and unnoticed.
Free of the unshakable terror that made me write . . .
I pick it up, a head holy and unholy,
tonsured or damaged,
with gross black charcoaled brows and stern eyes
frowning as if they had seen the splendor
times past counting . . . unspoiled,
solemn as a child is serious—
light balsa wood the color of my skin.
It is all childcraft, especially
its shallow, chiseled ears,
crudely healed scars lumped out
to listen to itself, perhaps, not knowing
it was made to be given up.
Goodbye nothing. Blockhead,
I would take you to church,
if any church would take you . . .
This winter, I thought
I was created to be given away.

Epilogue

Those blessèd structures, plot and rhyme—
why are they no help to me now
I want to make
something imagined, not recalled?
I hear the noise of my own voice:
The painter's vision is not a lens,
it trembles to caress the light.
But sometimes everything I write
with the threadbare art of my eye
seems a snapshot,
lurid, rapid, garish, grouped,
heightened from life,
yet paralyzed by fact.
All's misalliance.
Yet why not say what happened?
Pray for the grace of accuracy
Vermeer gave to the sun's illumination
stealing like the tide across a map
to his girl solid with yearning.
We are poor passing facts,
warned by that to give
each figure in the photograph
his living name.

Translations

Rabbit, Weasel, and Cat

(Adapted from La Fontaine)

Dame Weasel one fine morning stole
into young Rabbit's furnished hole;
it was an easy trick to play,
the master had stepped out to pay
his courtship to Aurora and the day,
and taste the clover and the dew.
Gobbling all that he could chew,
the rabbit trots home to his burrow—
the weasel's nose is pointing through the window.
The dislodged rabbit gives a shout,
"My God, what's this? This needle-snout?
Dame Weasel, leave, you have no choice,
don't make me raise my voice—
shall I call out the rats?"
The weasel answers, "Property
belongs to the present occupant.
An ignoble *casus belli*,
this hole I can only enter on my belly—
suppose it were Versailles!
Tell me, Friend, on what condition
is a holding handed down
to John or Henry's son,
or you, and not to me?"
The rabbit cited religion and tradition.
"There's law," he said, "that renders me
binding dominion of this habitation.
It came from James and Peter down to me.
The first possessor, is there better law?"
"Let's go then to an honest judge,"
Dame Weasel answered, "to Rabinagruge."
This old cat lived in sanctity,
a holy man of a cat,

pudgy and sleek-furred
from sipping at his pot of fat—
an expert in legality.
"Come nearer, Children," the old cat purred;
"I'm deaf, alas, for who can fight the years?"
The litigants came close, they had no fears.
Seeing them stand within arm's reach,
the cat plopped a soft paw on each,
and by breaking their necks, made peace.
This is the fate
of little nations that appeal to great.

George III

(This too is perhaps a translation, because I owe so much to Sherwin's brilliant Uncorking Old Sherry, *a life of Richard Brinsley Sheridan.—R.L.)*

Poor George,
afflicted by two Congresses,

ours and his own that regularly
and legally had him flogged—

once young George, who saw
his lost majority of our ancestors

dwindle to a few inglorious Tory refugee
diehards who fled for him to Canada—

to lie relegated to the ash-heap,
unvisited in this bicentennial year—

not a lost cause, but no cause.

In '76, George was still King George,
the one authorized tyrant,

not yet the mad, bad old king,

who whimsically picked the pockets of his page
he'd paid to sleep all day outside his door;

who dressed like a Quaker, who danced a minuet
with his appalled apothecary in Kew Gardens;

who did embroidery with the young court ladies,
and criticized them with suspicious bluntness;

who showed aversion for Queen Charlotte, almost
burned her by holding a candle to her face.

It was his sickness, not lust for dominion
made him piss purple, and aghast

his retinue by formally bowing to an elm,
as if it were the Chinese emissary.

George—

once a reigning monarch like Nixon,
and more exhausting to dethrone . . .

Could Nixon's court,
could Haldeman, Ehrlichman, or Kissinger

blame their king's behavior
on an insane wetnurse?

Tragic buffoonery
was more colorful once;

yet how modern George is,
wandering vacated chambers of his White House,

addressing imaginary congresses,
reviewing imaginary combat troops,

thinking himself dead and ordering black clothes:
in memory of George, for he was a good man.

Old, mad, deaf, half-blind,

he talked for thirty-two hours
on everything, everybody,

read Cervantes and the Bible aloud
simultaneously with shattering rapidity . . .

Quand on s'amuse, que le temps fuit—

in his last lucid moment,
singing a hymn to his harpsichord,

praying God for resignation
in his calamity he could not avert . . .

mercifully unable to hear
his drab tapes play back his own voice to him,

morning, noon, and night.

Arethusa to Lycotas

(*Propertius, Book IV, 3*)

Arethusa sends her Lycotas this command:
if I can call you, always absent, mine.
If some letters have an uncertain outline,
they're proofs I write you with a dying hand.

Bactra twice-visited, you rushed to see
the taunting Neurican on his armored horse,
the wintry Getae, Britain's painted cars,
the sunburnt Hindo by his sultry sea.

Is this our marriage? Hymen was gone when I
a stranger to love, and afraid of freedom, chose
the ominous torch that lit me to your house—
the coronet on my hair was set awry.

May whoever cut tentstakes from the harmless ash,
or carved the hoarse-complaining trumpet from bone—
die worse than Ocnus, who sits aslant to twine
his rope in hell forever to feed the ass.

Does the breastplate bruise your soft white flesh,
are your civil hands blistered by the war spear?
Better these hurt you than some girl should scar
your neck with toothmarks for my tears to heal.

Now sharper nights attend the evening star,
the blanket will not stay put on my bed—
I could kiss your dull weapons you left here dead . . .
the birds, that herald morning, sing no more.

I know the painted world of maps, I know
which way the Araxes you will ford must flow,
how far without water a Parthian horse will fly—
I've placed your almost polar city, Dai.

I know which lands the sun hurts, which the frost—
which wind will blow you home to Italy.
My older sister and old nurse swear to me
it's only the heavy winter holds you fast.

Hippolyta was lucky, she could enter the ring
barebreasted; a captain's helmet hid her curls.
I wish our Roman camps admitted girls,
I'd be faithful baggage for your soldiering.

Mountains would not frighten me with height,
or Jupiter chaining the high streams with ice.
All love is great—a wife has greater love,
Venus blows on this flame that it may live.

All's dead here—at rare Kalends, a lonely housemaid
opens the Lares on her perfunctory round;
I wait for the whine of Craugus, the small hound;
he is only claiming your place in my bed.

If the barn-owl scream from the neighboring oak,
or wine is sprinkled on the spluttering lamps,
that day requires we kill the first-year lambs;
blackmail hurries the stately priest to work.

I've no cause to shine in bridal attire,
make crystals glitter like waterdrops on my ears;
I hang shrines with flowers, the crossroad with green firs;
marjoram crackles in the ancestral fire.

Is glory taking Bactra's walls by force,
or tearing the turban from a perfumed king,
while the bow twangs from their hypocrite flying horse,
and lead scatters like hailstones from the twisted sling?

When their young men are gone, and slavery heals
their widows, and the spear without a head
drags at your triumphant horse's heels—
remember the vow that binds you to our bed.

If you come back to me by day or night,
and make us for the moment man and wife,
I'll bring your arms to the Capua Gate, and write:
From a girl grateful for her husband's life.

9 780374 514716